UNCHAINING THE
CHAIN OF COMMAND

Unchaining the Chain of Command

Paul Rubinyi

Crisp Publications

Editor-in-Chief: *William F. Christopher*
Project Editor: *Kay Keppler*
Editor: *Amy Marks*
Cover Design: *Kathleen Barcos*
Cover Production: *Russell Leong Design*
Book Design & Production: *London Road Design*
Printer: *Bawden Printing*

Copyright © 1998 by Crisp Publications, Inc.

All rights reserved. No part of this book may be reproduced or transmitted in any form or by any means now known or to be invented, electronic or mechanical, including photocopying, recording, or by any information storage or retrieval system without written permission from the author or publisher, except for the brief inclusion of quotation in a review.

Library of Congress Card Catalog Number 97-68249

ISBN 1-56052-440-5

Contents

Editor's Preface		vii
Author's Preface		ix
I.	Introduction to System Thinking	1
	Terminology	1
	Reinventing Corporate Leadership	3
	A Conceptual Base for System Thinking	5
II.	Managing the "Whole"	19
	The Concept of Corporate Management	21
	Direction and Integration	26
	Definition of Corporate Management	31
III.	A System Model for Corporate Management	33
	Level 1. Business Unit	38
	Level 2. The Corporate Integrating Channel	43
	Level 3. Corporate Business Management	46
	Level 4. The Management of Corporate Future-Related Activities	49
	Level 5. The Highest Management Authority of the Corporation	52
	Constructing the System Model	57
IV.	Corporate Management Role and Functions	63
	Role	64
	Core Functions	65
	Corporate Management Positions	69
	Summary and Conclusions	72

V.	PROJECTS	75
	Corporate Management Requirements	78
	Specific Project Management Requirements	80
	Audit	87
VI.	SUMMARY AND CONCLUSIONS	89
	Conclusions	91
APPENDIX: VSM		97
REFERENCES		99
FURTHER READING		101
ABOUT THE AUTHOR		103

Editor's Preface

This book applies the wisdom of general system science and cybernetics to the management of business enterprise. New wisdom is rare, seminal. The wisdom of general system theory and cybernetics, discovered and developed over the past half century, is one of these seminal events. Among the pioneers of this new science, Stafford Beer developed his Viable System Model (VSM) and applied it in business enterprise, government and nonprofit organizations in Europe and North and South America. Its application validated its value. Many experts contend that system science will become the integrating management philosophy for the future.

Paul Rubinyi, often working with Dr. Beer, applied system thinking and his version of the VSM in his consulting work with many corporations, government agencies and other organizations. This book describes what he learned over a successful career applying the new wisdom of system science.

I edited *Unchaining the Chain of Command* from a manuscript that Dr. Rubinyi was writing at the time of his death. Since the manuscript was only partly completed, I also used other papers and documents Dr. Rubinyi wrote, my experience working with him and with Dr. Beer applying their system science concepts in the large corporation I then worked for, as well as our contacts and correspondence over the years.

Editor's Preface

System science, system modeling and cybernetics provide a framework, and a design for information feedback, that executive management can use to build a successful enterprise in today's competitive, complex world.

Problems within a company system result from systemic dysfunctions, or changes in the external environment which can produce both problems and opportunities. These problems and opportunities can be dealt with best by fixing or adjusting the system. But we have to first "see" our organization as a system and understand the laws of system behavior. This book will help provide this view and this understanding.

I have learned a lot from Paul and Stafford. And I have applied this learning in businesses in a dozen countries—always with success. I hope what Paul has written of his experience will be helpful to you. Read Stafford's books, too, as Paul recommends and cites as references. System science is real; it exists. It will shape our futures by our choice, or unrecognized and unused, by chance and by surprise.

William F. Christopher
Editor

Author's Preface

Can the chain of command really be unchained? Many readers may already be thinking that "flatter is better." But they look at their companies and see a traditional management pyramid and the chain of command that goes with it. How can this chain of command be unchained; decisions made quickly where and when needed; the enterprise more productive, more responsive, a better place to work? System science and system thinking shows us a way.

A change in corporate life is not a matter of choice. At least three underlying factors make fundamental change necessary for company success:

- Corporate management must respond to opportunities and threats that are new, different, unexpected and much greater in their impact.

- Today's economic and social life has become so complex that coping with the changes requires new management approaches.

- The emergence of globalization has greatly expanded the scope of management.

In most corporations the search is on for developing the best approaches to corporate management under the new conditions. Current business literature, newspapers, magazines and my own experience support the view that currently there are many problems in executive management. Some corporate executive groups are still focusing on financial control. Others are acting only as investors and are neglecting other management functions. Some top managements have introduced full decentralization and have lost corporate synergy benefits. Some others are still very reluctant to provide meaningful autonomy to the operating units. And others believe the remedy is cost-cutting, and keep the organization in a permanent state of reconstruction.

The systems approach described and advocated in this book replaces the traditional management hierarchy with a web (not a maze) of operating units having autonomous management and integrating forces that link them into the total company. With unchaining, corporate management becomes the designer and integrator of the total company system. The business units are self-managed enterprises, operating within corporate guidelines and constraints. They are not simply decentralized operations. They survive and prosper primarily on their own but also with the support of the total system of which they are component parts. And in their work they contribute to the goals of the total system, the company.

With the proposed approach, the budget of a self-managed business unit serves the needs of the management of that unit and need not be "approved" by corporate management. When the unit is established, corporate management provides resources and from time to time issues policy statements and financial directives. In traditional companies no approval of the budget by

AUTHOR'S PREFACE

corporate management sounds like a revolution. When I suggested this approach for a firm with 54 subsidiary companies around the globe, and with corporate headquarters approving quarterly budgets for each of them, the CEO strongly opposed it. "You would take away my basic control device. I would never agree to this as long as I am in command here." A few years later, the company's central control was not able to cope with the new, changing environment.

The approach described in this book recognizes a structure of viable business systems, corporate synergies, and the need for discipline. This is a world of coordinated, self-managed systems operating within a total company system, which is very different from the traditional organization pyramid. This management approach is called "indirect management."

Indirect management is the opposite of "direct management." Direct management makes specific decisions on lower-level matters, in a relationship between superior and subordinate in a hierarchical management structure. Indirect management is exercised by the management of a higher-level system over component operating systems. Indirect management is based on the view that a component system is a "black box" from the standpoint of the management of the higher-level system. By definition, then, the higher-level management has no competence in the operational details of the lower-level system. The behavior of the black box can be observed, its inputs controlled, its results measured, its boundaries and functions determined, but management of the larger system cannot enter into the black box operations . . . unless it gives up its leadership position. The relationship between corporate management and the management of operating units is that of a business partnership, operating within corporate parameters.

Indirect management recognizes that the business world, as in nature, is structured as a hierarchy of dynamic systems. Each business system in the hierarchy has both self-asserting tendencies and integrating links with the higher-level business system.

Each business system has a full range of management functions corresponding to the scope of management involved. Corporate management deals with matters that the operating units could not handle, such as planning the corporation's portfolio of businesses. And a business unit management, for example, might plan for market penetration in a given business.

Top management's basic means for applying indirect management are as follows:

- determining the total organization's basic business concept and the basic mandates or missions of the component operating units

- appointing or discharging the heads of the lower-level units

- designing and implementing corporate parameters to be observed by the component businesses

- allocating corporate resources initially as endowment and later to new projects or increased working capital needs

Author's Preface

The change from direct to indirect management also reflects the changing preferences of people. Networking is replacing the chain of command. In advanced organizations there is a tendency to dismantle middle management levels, procedures and rules that might once have been justified but now contribute to the preservation of outmoded and harmful management practices.

Indirect management will require a change in the thoughts and practices of higher-level management. The center of interest will shift from controlling and supervising operations to the production of added value by the total organization. Top management will become much more conceptual. It will deal with aggregates, abstractions, strategy formulations and so on. Hands-on management will still be needed, but the hands of the corporate managers will be on levers that mobilize synergetic resources rather than on the details of lower-level operations. Corporate managers will concentrate on managing the whole, rather than on managing the parts.

Executives are searching for the right modus operandi for corporate management. I strongly believe that these executives have the capability of meeting the new challenges, helped in their search by the concepts described in this book.

In writing this book I am indebted to many business people from whom I obtained practical experience. I am also indebted to many writers, teachers and academicians who added meaning to the experience. This learning, and my work with clients over more than three decades of consulting, have provided me with experiences and observations confirming what I advocate in this book.

Author's Preface

I want to express my greatest gratitude to Stafford Beer, who was my advisor in my Ph.D. studies for managerial cybernetics at Brunel University in London. I continued learning from him in my consulting work. Dr. Beer and I worked together on many consulting engagements over a period of two decades. We rarely agreed on anything, but our joint effort always produced high-quality services and client satisfaction. The concepts and methods described in this book have improved performance in many organizations. Here I wish to give full credit to Dr. Beer for what I learned from him and the ideas that inspired me in writing this book. The knowledge I gained from him helped me develop a new understanding of past and present business experience through applying general systems notions—a total, holistic approach to business. I also learned much of system thinking from Russell Ackoff, Arthur Koestler, Ludwig von Bertalanffy and Norbert Wiener.

My academic training and management practices have been obtained in two different social systems: in Hungary (1945–56) and in Canada (from 1957). I arrived in Canada as a well-educated Marxist (Ph.D. in Marxian Economics and two years in a political academy) with ten years of experience in executive positions in the Hungarian Soviet-type government. I thought that in Canada I would never be able to use my business training and academic background obtained in Hungary. It turned out that I was overly pessimistic. Although a prevailing social system can greatly retard or enhance managerial effectiveness, life taught me that business experience gained–good or bad–always provides valuable lessons for management development.

Corporate management practices are in a state of transition. The changes needed are only beginning to be made. Among us all we have to create the new management practices. The field is wide open for experimentation and learning.

This book is written for people who recognize that corporate management–the management of the total enterprise–is a new kind of job with a new orientation, a new way of working. This book describes some powerful concepts for this new corporate management job. I hope it provides some useful information and motivation for present and future corporate managers.

Paul Rubinyi
Montréal

I.

Introduction to System Thinking

THIS BOOK OFFERS EXECUTIVES responsible for corporate leadership a box of tools from the discipline of system thinking. Using these tools, management can unchain the chain of command, strengthen control and improve performance results. For a preliminary orientation, this chapter discusses three topics: terminology, reinventing corporate leadership, and a conceptual base for system thinking.

Terminology

Corporate

The term "corporate" refers to a total situation that can be characterized as a whole. A corporate whole is a dynamic business system that has interacting operating units. Such a corporate whole can produce added values more than the sum of values produced by the operating units individually. A large organization may have a number of corporate wholes depending on the critical influence-centers of the web of operating business units. The whole and the parts are indeed very relative terms.

Management

Management is viewed as a force that integrates human effort. Management obtains, employs, combines and operates the key resources of labor (human resources), land (natural resources), and capital (man-made resources), in order to achieve desired ends.

This definition has basic implications. It determines the nature of management effort. Management focus is not concentrated on profit maximization, maximization of shareholder value or maximization of executive wealth. Instead the focus is on the role of the enterprise to satisfy customers and the needs of society for which it is rewarded with profit to be distributed to stakeholders in a balanced way.

Management and leadership are inseparable, but they are not the same. Managers must be effective at both. A manager who cannot lead is not a manager. A leader who cannot manage is not a leader. The distinction between leadership and management is a matter of scope. Leadership determines desired ends, governs the basic aspects of management activities and provides inspiration for their accomplishment. Management materializes leadership.

The tasks of leadership and the scope of management depend on the nature and level of the business system in the system hierarchy. In any discussion the level of management involved must be identified correctly.

Corporate management. Corporate management is a distinct level of management responsible for the overall results and progress of an organization formed by component units.

Corporate leadership. Corporate leadership includes the board of directors, the top corporate management team and the corporate headquarters staff.

Corporate leadership system. Corporate leadership is more than a single individual or even a group of individuals. Making decisions and taking actions involves many participants and support systems, communication and information channels, and processes of discovery and rationalization. These elements together form the corporate leadership system.

Executive business managers and operating business managers. This book distinguishes between two types of managers. Executive business managers integrate human efforts and obtain, employ and combine the key resources of the business. Operating business managers carry out actual business transactions. Neither category is better than the other. They require different expertise. The executive manager creates the business; the operating manager carries out the business activities.

Reinventing Corporate Leadership

Reinvention is a process that transforms an existing system into a new, different system. The new system is not developed from scratch. It evolves from the old one. In a successful enterprise the process is difficult, painful and evolutionary. In a failing enterprise it is revolutionary . . . if the enterprise is to transform successfully.

There is a difference between reinventing and restructuring a business. Reinventing starts with the following question: "Under the present and coming realities and trends, what is the business and how should we go about creating it?" Restructuring, in contrast, focuses on productivity and profitability issues for preserving and improving the existing system. In many cases, restructuring has deteriorated into a cost-cutting exercise and at best produces an improved performance of the existing business.

We are living and working in an era of reinventing the whole industrial world. Corporate management is confronted with challenges and opportunities that earlier management groups have not faced, including:

- fast-changing and unforgiving markets
- globalization
- deregulation
- moving from mechanistic to holistic, entrepreneurial organizations
- fundamental changes in the preferences of people
- increased structural unemployment
- the emergence of working at home, linked to business associates by computers and telecommunications
- the changing role of women

- the changing structure of society

To deal with these challenges and opportunities, new initiatives are needed that can be launched only from the highest level of management. Only the highest level has the necessary vantage point and the authority needed to make fundamental directional decisions, and employ and redeploy corporate resources. New management methods and approaches will be needed. The reinvention of corporate leadership tasks, approaches and methods is under way!

A Conceptual Base for System Thinking

Four basic concepts can help guide top management through the reinvention process:

- The prime function of the enterprise is to produce value for customers and benefits for society. In exchange, the enterprise receives monetary rewards for services rendered.

- The management approach chosen by corporate management has a great social significance.

- The management of complexity at the corporate level calls for a new kind of leadership system.

- The firm is a complex, dynamic system governed in a fundamental way by the natural laws that drive such systems.

  Let's examine each of these concepts in more depth.

The prime function of the enterprise is to produce value for customers and benefits for society. In exchange, the enterprise receives monetary rewards for services rendered.

According to this concept the enterprise performs a service for customers and a social role in society, and earns financial rewards in return. The perception of the firm is a highly practical matter to corporate managers. Different perceptions lead to different identities, different management practices, different structures, and different results.

People do have different perceptions of the enterprise. For example, an engineer may view the firm as a production capacity, a customer may view it as a provider of certain products or services, a lawyer as a legal entity, an accountant as a chart of accounts and a set of books, a programmer as a set of algorithms, an economist as an econometric model, a psychologist as a group of people who have certain behavioral characteristics, a financial analyst as an investment opportunity, a purchasing agent as a supplier, a politician as a source of votes and financial support, an employee as the foundation of his or her livelihood and so on. These perceptions are valid but not very helpful to a corporate manager who tries to lead all members of the enterprise toward a mutually accepted, ultimate purpose.

These different perceptions are here to stay. They cannot be changed, nor do they need to change. Life has many faces. Corporate management has the task of working together with people who have different perceptions.

The full utilization of the company's resources calls for an agreed-upon view and perception about the basic nature of the company and its principal functions, understanding that individuals have their own views about their respective interests.

Many people in the business world perceive the enterprise as an instrument to make profit and to increase shareholders' wealth. From the standpoint of the investor, this may be a valid statement. Various methodologies for measuring the value of a company consider only the financial aspects and have little or no interest in the firm's business activities. There is an underlying belief that the "bottom line" expresses everything.

The bottom line is not the only thing that counts. The view that the company is an instrument with which to make profit is a narrow-minded perception and not sufficient for corporate managers. It obscures important functions of corporate management and the entire corporate leadership system. Corporations, led by corporate managers, combine and control the key resources of a nation. Corporate management has the task of obtaining and combining these resources to produce desired results. Corporations produce the bulk of the gross national product of all industrial nations.

A full understanding of the role of the company in the society will provide the broadest and most operationally meaningful view for managing the company. A common language will help corporate managers determine the identity and the mission of their organization. Corporate managers should know about society, politics, philosophy and macroeconomics; and they should be able to translate this knowledge into business advantages.

The management approach chosen by corporate management has a great social significance.

This concept emphasizes the social significance of the management approach chosen by corporate management. Large corporations influence the everyday lives of all members of the society. Every time a customer buys something, he or she votes on the performance of the companies that produce and distribute the product or service, and on the social system within which the companies exist and operate. The management approach can make a difference between creative managerial freedom and status quo bureaucracy, and between a modern adaptive organization and an organization mechanistically conceived.

The social consequences of a prevailing management approach have been pointed out by many authors, including Chandler (*The Invisible Hand: The Managerial Revolution in American Business*), Drucker (*The Frontiers of Management*), Naisbitt (*Reinventing the Corporation*), and Burnham (*The Managerial Revolution*). Burnham went as far as to say: "The theory of the managerial revolution predicts that capitalist society will be replaced by managerial society . . . that in fact, the transition from capitalist society to managerial society is already well under way."[1] I do not agree with Burnham's conclusion, but the issues raised well support the view that a managerial approach has a great social significance.

Corporate managers have a social responsibility. Once a management approach is generally established, it will directly affect profitability, shareholders' wealth, the everyday lives of people and the society's prosperity.

The social significance of a management approach can be illustrated by the Soviet example. Apart from any political consideration, it represented an extreme case of a mechanistically conceived organization. It was the ultimate bureaucratic creation. The population and the resources of the largest country in the world were locked into a fantastically complex and cumbersome superstructure that prohibited creativity, invited mediocrity and corruption, and produced a permanent shortage of basic necessities.

Corporate life demonstrates everywhere that the tighter the direction from above, the more unpleasant and unproductive the managerial world below. In the Soviet system, basic factors of the economy such as price, capital, money, cost and profit became administrative means instead of moving forces in the economy. The result was a very much underperforming economy. The Soviet system failed miserably to provide the basic necessities for its people. The entire revolutionary process going on in Russia, its former Soviets, and the Eastern European countries is about the need for changing the entire managerial approach from a centralized structure to a market economy.

This point about the social significance of a management approach reinforces the first concept. The development of an effective corporate management approach calls for deep insight into the social forces at work in and around the organization, and an understanding of the role of the enterprise in society.

The management of complexity at the corporate level calls for a new kind of leadership system.

Corporate managers manage a very high degree of complexity. The variables affecting a large business are so numerous that they cannot be interrelated by one person's mental processes. Yet making informed decisions calls for a careful analysis and understanding of these variables and their interrelationships—a valid perception of the total picture. The situation calls for new devices and management techniques to extend human capabilities. This book recommends an approach that responds to this problem and offers ways and means to cope with the complexity of the total situation. The need for hands-on management is recognized, but what is critical is *what* corporate managers put their hands on.

Leadership of complex organizations is no longer simply a matter of a single extraordinary personality or even a group of such individuals. Leadership of complex organizations requires a system that certainly includes leaders whose personal qualities remain decisive in discharging leadership functions. But it also includes many other participants, management support systems, and a whole process of rationalization. A CEO, however talented, cannot directly control operations at lower levels. Business systems and leadership are needed at intermediate levels to provide this control.

The firm is a complex, dynamic system governed in a fundamental way by the natural laws that drive such systems.

This concept views the enterprise as a dynamic system that has unique governing forces. This book proposes system thinking as a guide and model for effective management. System thinking can be taught and learned. The emerging discipline of system science provides a unique source of management wisdom. It is a science for generalists. It discovers and describes general laws and performance characteristics common to all systems. We can learn the principles common to all systems and then apply them in managing complex organizations.

In a broad sense, system science is a very old science. If the term is defined as the exploration of the basic laws of nature and society, then all human knowledge could be included. This is not very practical, however. Here we talk about system science in a more restricted sense as it has developed over the past half century as the science of complex systems.

Ludwig von Bertalanffy, the founder of general system theory, underlined three aspects of this theory:

- system science proper, which is the exploration of systems for discovering principles that apply to all systems

- system technology, comprising hardware and software and the associated concepts and theories

- system philosophy, which provides a holistic view versus the reductionist view

In his book *General System Theory,* von Bertalanffy commented:

> . . . the system viewpoint has penetrated and has indeed proved indispensable in a vast variety of scientific and technological fields. This and the further fact that it represents a novel 'paradigm' in scientific thinking . . . has a consequence that the concept of system can be defined and developed in different ways as required by the objectives of research, and as reflecting different aspects of the central notion.[2]

Professor William J. Reckmeyer has briefly and eloquently described the development and short history of system science:

> Nearly thirty years have elapsed since the basic ideas and insights of the general system field were first proposed in a fairly explicit fashion by Wiener, von Bertalanffy, Ashby, Boulding, von Foerester, McCulloch and several other perceptive scholars from a variety of diverse disciplinary backgrounds. Spurning the narrow perspectives of their respective disciplines and sharing a common conviction concerning the inherently unified nature of reality, they all recognized the compelling need for an appropriately broad approach to understanding and dealing with the complexity of the world, and began to develop a meta ('over and above') disciplinary perspective on reality that emphasized the intrinsic order and interdependence of the world in all of its manifestations.[3]

Unfortunately, system science notions have been slow to penetrate into the business world. Some of the advanced management schools teach them, but business people know little about them.

A typical managerial situation can be viewed as a dynamic system as defined by system science, with parts in interaction, for a purpose, in an environment in which events occur, and whose state changes over time. The aspects that are common to all systems suggest some basic forces at work that operate independently from human will. These basic forces are the workings of natural laws. Adam Smith called such laws "invisible hands." Arthur Koestler described them as "ghosts in the machine." The natural laws of system science govern, regulate and affect life in general and in organizations.

The teachings of system science are very much applicable to management, especially to corporate management. Many of the views, methods and techniques described in this book have their origin in system science. Stafford Beer pioneered the application of system science to management. This book and many others on the subject were greatly influenced by Dr. Beer's writings and teachings.

Some authors believe that the application of system science to management transforms management from art to science. I disagree with this view. The human factor will remain the dominating essence of management. I don't believe in scientific management. But I believe very much in the application of science in management.

When one studies the discoveries of system science and the application of these discoveries in management, the findings sometimes seem obvious. For example, the discovery that a whole can do things that a part cannot do may seem far from earthshaking. Managers already know this concept, or think they do. But in my experience, very few leaders truly focus their attention on the total picture and on the utilization of the synergetic capabilities inherent only in the total organization. Many leaders and managers may want to have such a focus but have no idea how to go about doing so. Instead they involve themselves with matters that can be handled better at a lower level of management.

System thinking can help corporate managers:

- identify a total organization and gain an overview of it
- identify the component operating units of the total organization
- recognize patterns and trends
- identify and recognize basic relationships
- identify synergetic potentials

System thinking also:

- sets a limit as to what is possible
- suggests ways of organizing the management process
- is conducive to designing the development of a total organization

This book offers some novel concepts, methods and techniques to support an emerging type of corporate management that will unchain the chain of command, enabling an organization to:

- replace the control-and-command principle with systemic relationships, teamwork, self-coordination and common value systems
- focus on the total picture, the overall design
- apply indirect management and macro approaches
- not try to know, understand and control all details of the organization
- not be addicted to figures
- concentrate on the utilization of capabilities intrinsic only to the total organization
- let the operators operate at a very high degree of freedom within the corporate parameters
- operate without an elaborate chain of command between corporate management and the operators

Following is a preview of some of the novel notions discussed in this book (see Figure 1):

- Corporate management is a unique producing unit rather than an overhead item. This level of management does things that cannot be done at the levels of the corporate operating units.
- Indirect management replaces a control-and-command approach with systemic relationships.

- Directional planning should precede strategic planning; otherwise, strategy will define its own objectives.

- All planned changes must be accounted for by projects. The movement of projects from definition to completion is the most fundamental aspect of managerial planning.

- Each management group in the web of organizational units must be able to plan without receiving written plans from above or below.

- There should be a balance between corporate development and corporate operating management. Within the top team, clear responsibilities should be assigned for focusing on both.

- People who are trained and experienced functionally may not perceive the totality of the organization; therefore, no one should be in the top team without direct profit responsibilities.

Figure 1 visualizes the general scenario developed in this book.

Introduction to System Thinking

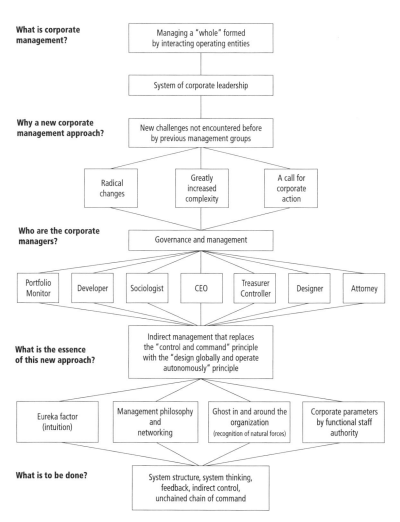

Figure 1. A scenario for managing large systems without a chain of command

II.

Managing the "Whole"

CORPORATE MANAGEMENT IS A distinct level of management responsible for the overall results and position of a complex organization. Such an organization is formed by operating units, each with its own management, and each an integral part of a larger system—the corporate organization. Effective corporate management manages the whole, without managing the parts. It does not violate the principle of autonomous operating management.

This concept sounds simple enough, but it is not well understood. In many cases the corporate "management of the whole" is not articulated as such and is usually underdeveloped. Corporate management as defined in this book usually does not appear in the organization chart. Instead we see terms such as top management, headquarters or parent, or the names and titles of top executives. When and where the concept of corporate management of the whole is fully understood, the new perception will likely cause drastic change in management practices.

High-level corporate managers know that they have a very special management task. They may be overwhelmed by it. A newly appointed chief executive officer (CEO) promoted from a specific area of responsibility (finance or marketing) or from a lower level of management (managing an operating unit with direct control over operations) can be overwhelmed when he or she encounters the corporate complexities. These complexities include:

- several corporate functions, such as finance, research and human resources, each with its own technology and jargon
- operating units engaged in different businesses and located in various parts of the world
- differing national characteristics and changing exchange rates
- different technologies essential for corporate success
- people with different cultural and academic backgrounds
- variations in the size of the corporation's businesses and the magnitude of money involved
- geographic distances
- legal requirements in different countries and jurisdictions

How can one cope with these complexities? In my consulting practice, I have seen three kinds of reactions from newly appointed CEOs:

- The CEO senses the complexity, is overwhelmed by it, and continues to do what he or she was good at before, thus interfering with someone else's job and leaving the corporate job unattended.

- The CEO senses the complexity and is overwhelmed but pretends to carry out the job, even though he or she remains uninvolved and uncommitted, and runs away from decision-making. Again, the corporate job is left unattended.

- The CEO realizes that this is a new job and calls for a new orientation, a new learning curve and the use of all the experience he or she has but in a different way and on a different scale.

This book was written for people in this third group. For these people, this chapter explains the nature of corporate management conceptually, as a dynamic system, and functionally.

The Concept of Corporate Management

As described in Chapter I, the term "corporate" refers to a total situation, a whole that is formed of interacting, dynamic components. In a large organization the business hierarchy may include a number of corporate situations and corporate management groups. For example, a large international industrial organization may have several corporate headquarters: world, regional, company, profit center (within a company) and plant (within a profit center).

Misconceptions About Corporate Management

This book focuses on corporate management at an elevated level in a business system, responsible for the results and progress of the organization as a whole. There are many misconceptions about the nature of corporate management. Discussing some of these misconceptions will help us come up with a general definition of corporate management.

Corporate management = central financial control. Under this perception, the corporation's component operating units receive a very limited amount of business direction. Central financial control dictates only financial standards and requirements for the operating units and records transactions that have already happened. This type of control deals with history. When financial control dominates corporate management, the operating executives view corporate management as a holding company.

Corporate management = portfolio management. Business portfolio management considers the capital tied up in each distinct business of the corporation and the earnings by which the individual businesses contribute to the corporation's total earnings. Corporate business portfolio management can and in many cases does produce added values for the organization. It is a very important activity. However, when the management of the business portfolio dominates, and corporate management is involved mainly in making acquisitions, mergers and other deals, the operational synergies of the organization may not be fully utilized. When the majority of the senior officer's time is absorbed by business portfolio management, it creates the impression that the whole company is an instrument to make profit and is nothing more than a bundle of assets to be manipulated as investments. This environment is not very motivating for the operating managers and operating people. Business portfolio management is a key activity but only one function of corporate management.

Corporate management = ranks. The presence of ranks does not mean that the corporate management is doing its job. An organization may have a chairman, president, CEO and senior vice presidents, but they may perform only some of the corporate management functions. Rather than providing leadership, they may spend much of their time acting on matters that are passed up to them for decisions, intervening in work better left to others.

Corporate management = ringmaster function. Top management sometimes is called on to be a tiebreaker between managers who hold differing views and whose planned or actual actions cause conflicts. Often such conflicts arise between corporate staff and field operating people. Corporate management has both the authority and the function to act as a tiebreaker when it is called for. But if this happens too many times, it indicates structural problems. Corporate management has the task of designing and providing an operating management framework that can stimulate and coordinate voluntary interactions between organization units. This will keep conflicting situations at a minimum.

Corporate management = ownership. This perception prevails especially when the owner—a family owner or an owner-manager through leveraged buyout—is physically present. The entrepreneur-owner may create the enterprise and establish whatever management practices suit his or her own personal characteristics and abilities. Seldom is there true corporate management. When ownership results from a leveraged management buyout, the shareholders are the management group. Typically these are operating managers who may or may not establish effective corporate management.

Ownership alone does not form an organization or create corporate management. Organizations are formed by business relationships. Ownership functions and management functions are not the same. Owner-managers may carry out both functions but should be conscious of their differences.

Corporate management = centralization. Centralization does not mean the exercise of true corporate management. In a centralized decision process, the decision makers may make decisions on matters one by one as they are submitted to them from below. Many of these decisions would be better made at lower levels. Centralization gives an illusion of being in control. But the organization may be fragmented, with its parts drifting in conflicting directions.

Centralization means retaining decision authority at a higher level. Decentralization delegates decision authority to where the work is done. Integration—a task of corporate management—links operating units for the benefit of the enterprise as a whole. Experience shows that effective decentralization requires an effective overall integration. Integration can be accomplished with either centralization or decentralization. But corporate management does not centralize anything the operating units should do. It centralizes things that cannot be done by lower-level management.

Corporate management = overhead. Lower-level management may not see or understand the role of corporate management, considering it as overhead. When corporate expenses are allocated to the operating units, the unit managers believe they are paying for uncontrolled "corporate overhead." There is no good reason to allocate corporate expenses to the operating units. Operating management is responsible only for revenues and expenses under its control. Allocation of corporate costs goes against this principle. Corporate management adds value and becomes a producing unit. It should keep its own accounting. If corporate management does not exercise its true role, then it is rightly considered overhead.

Corporate management = resource to operating managers. The managers of the operating units usually want to discuss some of their business problems and opportunities with higher-level management. This is normal, and corporate managers should avail themselves. But, sometimes, this is the only thing corporate managers do. The interaction between the two levels of management then deteriorates to a "big brother" approach, and corporate management fails to attend to its real job—directing the entire organization.

Direction and Integration

Many of the perceptions described above are part of corporate management. But each of these perceptions is only one aspect of this level of management. There is a broader responsibility. Corporate management has the basic and important responsibility for two streams of activities that only they can handle:

- ensuring the full utilization of the capabilities inherent only in the total organization
- integrating all components of the organization to ensure unity in action and purpose for the entire organization

The essence of corporate management is that it directs and integrates the organization as a whole to create more than the sum of its parts. In systems science, the whole and the sum are very different notions. Let's discuss the two streams of activities listed above that only corporate management can handle, beginning with the first of these: ensuring the full utilization of the capabilities inherent only in the total organization.

In system science, a dynamic whole is viewed as an open, dynamic system with components that interact. A change in any component affects all other components. The whole cannot be explained simply by analyzing the characteristics of the parts since it is the interaction among the components that creates the whole. The interaction is present only in the whole. It is not present in the components.

The sum is the total of the components. A change in an element depends on and affects only that element. A change in the sum is the sum of all changes in all elements.

These are important teachings for corporate management. An organization as a whole, the corporate whole, has its own characteristics that cannot be explained by the characteristics of the component operating units. An investigation of the physical and chemical properties of the parts of a refrigerator will not reveal that the machine as a whole can produce a desired temperature. The whole has capabilities that are intrinsic only to the total organization and are not possessed by the parts. One of the prime roles of corporate management is to foster and strengthen total corporate capabilities rather than focus its effort on interfering in the next level of management.

The very existence of an organization is justified only if it does something that is desired and that the component parts cannot do. Where such corporate capabilities are not present, corporate management is usually harmful to the business activities of the organizational units.

For the individual craftsman in the Middle Ages who used and owned his own hammer and chisel, the production process did not need an organization. When these hand tools were replaced by steam-driven machine tools and production became technologically socialized, an organization was then necessary. And when an organization is required, corporate management is needed to identify, exploit and foster the capabilities of the organization as a whole. Based on my consulting engagements, the following list of examples describes corporate capabilities inherent only in the total organization:

- overall financial strength and thus the ability to undertake and also to withstand risk involved in major business projects
- globalization—ability to divide work on an international scale and to do business wherever there is a profit opportunity
- agility to enter into a new business or to exit from an existing business without major disruption
- ability to shift resources (people, money or capacities) among operating units as the business situation may require
- ability to enter into undertakings that would not have been possible for an individual operating unit
- ability of an individual operating unit to perform business transactions that require the strength of the resources and organization of the total corporation of which the unit is a part
- ability of an international professional organization to provide standardized services at any location in the world through its international network of offices
- benefit of brand name identity possessed by a large organization that can dominate in a local market

- ability to purchase at more favorable costs and, in general, to employ the advantages of scale offered by the total organization
- ability to employ high-caliber experts

In general, these holistic capabilities are created by the interaction of the operating units and by specific resources employed at corporate headquarters. Corporate management has a prime function to identify, foster and utilize these capabilities.

Now we can turn to a discussion of the second stream of activities that is the responsibility of corporate management: integrating all of the components of the organization to ensure unity in action and purpose for the entire organization.

Integration links parts together for a common purpose. An organization has integrity if all component operating units contribute to the achievement of the total organization's purpose. Integration can be achieved by centralization, decentralization or, most productively, by systemic linkages. The systemic linkages create new relationships. This is the approach proposed in this book.

Corporate integration may hurt the interest of a component business. The head of such a business cannot be asked to do something that is good for the whole but detrimental to his or her component business. The corporate design should set corporate parameters that prevent or at least reduce these situations. This can usually be done by appropriate performance measures. Corporate integrating activities may include the following:

- determining the willed future of the organization
- providing financial resources
- designing the organization and the business infrastructure
- carrying out acquisition and merger activities and introducing new businesses into the total business system
- appointing key executives of the component business units
- determining the missions of the component units
- setting corporate goals and guidelines, and endowing and allocating resources
- evaluating business performance of the organization as a whole and of each operating unit
- setting corporate parameters that must be observed by all operating units
- networking with operating management

In carrying out the integrating activities, corporate management must be conscious of the fact that it cannot be competent in a wide variety of businesses, in different markets, and requiring a variety of disciplines. Two points should be added here:

- The scope of corporate activities is "macro" in nature. Corporate management should not go into all of the details.

- Corporate management needs a structure of management throughout the enterprise.

Definition of Corporate Management

Corporate management is a distinct level of management responsible for the overall results and position of an organization as a whole. It does things that cannot be done by lower-level management responsible for only one area of activity. The presence of corporate management is an objective necessity. Consider the following points:

- A business system as a whole has capabilities that are inherent only in the totality of the organization and are not possessed by the parts (overall financial strength; overall presence in the marketplace; synergistic gains from technology, knowledge, standardization, raw material supply, and multiple locations and the ability to undertake large projects). Corporate management is responsible for the organization as a whole and directs, integrates and compels the organization to achieve its holistic business potential.

- Certain managerial decisions can be made only by corporate management if suboptimization is to be avoided. Examples of such decisions include allocating resources to competing demands, appointing key managers and determining the identity of the organization. When such decisions emerge and the high-ranking corporate managers operate basically by a bottom-up approach, the organization drifts and its resources are underutilized. Corporate management ensures unity in purpose throughout the entire organization.

- Corporate management produces added value by making its own contribution to the overall strength of the organization and the results produced.

III.

A System Model for Corporate Management

CORPORATE MANAGEMENT PROVIDES leadership for a complex, large organization formed of operating units. Corporate management and operating units together make up the total business system. Corporate leadership must ensure the cohesion of the entire business system without diluting the creativeness of the management of the operating units. There is a useful model that helps us understand the nature of corporate management and its relations with the operating units.

Stafford Beer developed the model, and he described it in three of his books[4] and in many of his other publications and articles. Dr. Beer's model provides a systems way of looking at an organization. He named his model the Viable System Model (VSM). It is a model for all systems capable of living and succeeding in their environment.

Dr. Beer discovered the VSM through systematic study of the human nervous system and the generalization through mathematics of the principles found to relate to regulation. The rigorous mathematics were then transposed into rigorous diagrams, which is why Dr. Beer is so resolute in defense of his final pictograph of the VSM and its differences from the Rubinyi version, which I present in this book.

Dr. Beer's model has been applied by many professionals around the world with notable success. In my consulting practice I have applied my version of the model in more than eighty complex business and government organizations in various countries, also with success. I would like to acknowledge fully Dr. Beer's invention of the VSM and would also like to express my personal gratitude to him since he introduced me to the model and to system science.

The Rubinyi version of the model is similar to Dr. Beer's model in terms of its five-level system, its presentation (topography) and, to a large extent, its language. The differences in the model as I present it result from my own personal experiences in applying the model to corporate management, and its consequent adjustment to perceived managerial needs. I have continuously modified the original VSM to the version presented in this book. I have found the resulting Rubinyi model very useful in my own consulting practice, in helping executive leadership redefine and improve corporate management.

Dr. Beer points out—and I agree—that the model is much more than the diagram. The model presents a different way of thinking about organizations derived from systems science and cybernetics. My version of the model departs in some ways from the representations of these principles in the VSM. I include Dr. Beer's pictograph of the VSM in the Appendix. For detailed explanations of the VSM, refer to Dr. Beer's books, *Brain of the Firm, The Heart of Enterprise,* and *Diagnosing the System for Organizations.*

My use of the model describes a total business system as it is seen from above. It identifies managerial activities, the connecting links between them, and it suggests decision-making points. It describes the management organization as a five-level system that can be applied to any organization level. I have used this model to:

- explain the nature of corporate management
- define the component business units (next system level below corporate management)
- demonstrate that the organization is one large, dynamic, integrated system that is made up of operating units that demand a high degree of managerial autonomy
- determine the place of the various corporate management functions, and the corporate management positions, in the corporate management process
- define the roles and functions of corporate officers
- evaluate management practices
- improve communication between levels of management
- provide a model for designing an operationally meaningful information system

The term "systemic" differs from the term "systematic." Systematic means doing something by design with thoroughness and regularity. Systemic means pertaining to a larger system. A systemic hierarchy means that each system in the hierarchy subsumes the system below it. The systemic hierarchy has nothing to do with ranks and managerial hierarchy. You will see that someone operating at Level 1 in the systemic hierarchy may have a much higher managerial status than do many people at a higher system level. For instance, the head of a large operating unit is a Level 1 manager, and he or she may be a very high-level executive. We are discussing systemic levels and functions and not ranks and positions.

The model is a five-level system:

- Level 1 comprises the organization's component operating units. The operating units together with corporate management form the total business system.

- Level 2 is the corporate integrating and regulating mechanism that sets the basic requirements of the corporate game within which the Level 1 operating units should play the game. This level also coordinates the actions of Level 1 operating units.

- Level 3 refers to the overall business management of all the operating units.

- Level 4 indicates the center of managing future-related activities.

- Level 5 represents the highest level of management authority.

Levels 2, 3, 4 and 5 collectively become the corporate management system and individually represent the subprocesses. The model in its totality describes the integrating mechanism of a corporate organization.

By title, corporate executive positions do not convey the idea of system levels—corporate management without a chain of command. All members of the corporate executive group are involved in all levels of the systemic hierarchy. For example, as a member of the executive committee, a corporate vice president of human resources acts at Level 5 when he or she participates in executive committee decisions. The same executive would act at Level 4 when focusing on management development programs, and at Level 3 when assisting the CEO in finding and appointing a key operating executive. He or she will act at Level 2 when introducing corporate requirements on personnel matters to which the entire organization must adhere.

The model identifies the activities carried out by corporate management, as noted by the above example. In many organizations the members of the top management team are also responsible for certain bottom-line results. In this case the corporate manager has responsibilities at all five system levels, which helps the manager make informed decisions at the top.

A Level 1 operating unit can also be described by this five-level model. It has its own corporate management and component operating units. The scale and scope of the activities differ, but the basic pattern of management activities is the same. In a valid system model both subsystems and metasystems can be described by the same system model.

Level 1.
Business Unit

A business unit is a component operating unit of a larger business system that is perceived and viewed as such by top corporate management. The identification of the business units within a large organization is not a simple task. It involves judgment and a great deal of subjectivity. In many functionally structured organizations the organization chart does not even indicate the business units. They are there but are not perceived as business units. The determination of what constitutes the business units in a large organization is a crucial managerial decision that determines the fundamental corporate approach to business.

A business unit should have three characteristics:

- a distinct set of operations
- a distinct market (public)
- a distinct management

A complex business organization has a number of business units. A business unit may be an operational unit, a profit center division, a cost center, a subsidiary company, a geographic unit, a program headquarters, or a budget unit. The complexities in determining the business units of an organization can be seen in the following three examples.

> The corporate management of a very large insurance company may view its operating units in terms of the four "pillars" of the insurance industry: policy

development (actuarial activities), distribution (agent network), investment (investing the premiums and maintaining the reserve), and production (handling the paper flow associated with underwriting, policy administration and claim management). A very different perception would be to view the operations geographically (the Canada unit, the U.S. unit, the Caribbean unit, etc.). Defining the business units is a major task of corporate management.

A large international textile company determined that it is engaged in six different businesses. The company agonized for a long time over how to define the business units. Should each of the six be a worldwide business, or should geographic business units manage the six businesses in their respective areas? The company decided that one of the businesses would be a worldwide business unit and that geographic business units would manage the other five businesses.

Telephone companies traditionally were organized functionally (operations, finance, planning, etc.). New technology, deregulation and other business factors have caused telephone companies to restructure from functions to businesses. For example, residential service, business service, mobile operations and directory businesses became the operating units of telephone companies. This restructuring changed the responsibilities of both corporate management and operating management.

It is absolutely essential for corporate management to agree on the definition of the company's business units. Once this key issue is resolved, the entire corporate organization and the corporate management system can be established.

In determining the business units of an organization, I found useful the notions of system science and especially the notions put forward by Arthur Koestler. He emphasizes the hierarchical nature of the world of systems. Within the hierarchy, a given system is always part of a larger system and is itself formed of subordinate systems. A given system therefore is always a "whole" from the standpoint of its component systems, and a "part" from the standpoint of a larger system of which it is a part. Koestler searched for a term that could denote in one word this duality of a given system—a word including the ideas of both "whole" and "part." He invented the word, "holon," observing, "the term I would propose is holon from the Greek, *holos = whole,* with the suffix *on,* which, as in prot*on* or neutr*on*, suggests a particle or part."[5]

A business unit is a holon. It is a complete system in its own right, but it is also a part, a component of a larger system—the total corporate system, the larger holon.

In determining the business units and also deciding on their degree of autonomy, another system science notion that Koestler put forward needs to be considered. This notion is about the relationship between the integration of a total system and the self-asserting tendencies of the component units:

Every holon has a dual tendency to preserve and assert its individuality as a quasi-autonomous whole; and to function as an integrated part of a (existing or evolving) larger whole. This polarity between the Self-Assertive (S-A) and Integrative (INT) tendencies is inherent in the concept of hierarchy order and a universal characteristic of life.[6]

Koestler's observation is quite relevant to management. If the business unit is denied its self-assertive tendencies, the creativeness of its people will be weakened and the whole system will suffer. If corporate integration is not present or is weak, the system loses its synergetic potential and the business units drift. Corporate management must hit the right balance between two requirements—integration and self-assertion. One company decentralized without integrating and became an unorganized, underperforming corporation.

A business unit is linked to corporate management by three communication channels:

Business Channel. For everyday business communication and for decisions on resource allocation (such as for projects or increased working capital)

Integrating Channel. Through which corporate requirements are issued and received, coordinating information forwarded and received, and shared corporate services provided

Direct Personal Channel. For visits, telephone calls, social gatherings and so on

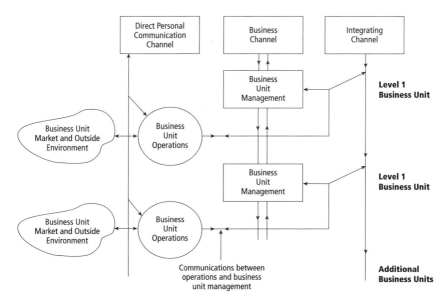

Figure 2. Level 1 business units with three channels of communication with corporate management

The concept of a business unit is illustrated in Figure 2.

For the business units, the receiving and forwarding points of these three communication channels are at two places: corporate headquarters and within the business unit's systems. Figure 2 conveys that at the business unit level the operators request decisions from their management through two-way communication channels. The business unit management receives and provides communication to and from corporate management through the business, integrating and direct personal channels. The communication channels shown here, and in the following diagrams of the other system levels, provide a model for the design of the company's information system.

Level 2.
The Corporate Integrating Channel

A business unit (Level 1) is a self-contained business organization that could survive in the market on its own. But it is also part of a larger system—the corporate system. The management of a business unit always intends to assert itself. This is expected and encouraged. But the linkages to the corporate management level are essential for both corporate management and operations management to utilize the synergetic capabilities of the entire system. The integrating channel is a key linkage between levels of management. It unifies, integrates and regulates the total organization.

The corporate integrating mechanism includes:

- routinized information flow, such as operating reports, financial data, regulatory reports and routine correspondence
- a balanced set of internal and external key indicators
- communication of corporate general parameters to be met by all business units
- certain shared corporate services

The selection of key indicators is a critical element of this integrating mechanism. Striking the appropriate balance between financial and nonfinancial measures, and between internally oriented and externally oriented measures is a vital task of corporate management.

It is essential to understand the nature of corporate parameters. A parameter is a corporate constant that management at all levels must observe. A parameter establishes basic requirements in a broad way. For instance, a chart of accounts determines the basic accounting requirements for the business units. But in applying this corporate chart of accounts, the business units are free to include further detailed accounts to record the particulars of their business activities. Furthermore, the posting of business transactions to the unit's own accounts is entirely a matter for the unit's accounting. The corporate chart of accounts is a corporate parameter. For example, when someone mentions an account number from the corporate chart of accounts, everybody should know what it means. The corporation's statement of ethical values is also a corporate parameter, as is the use of a corporate logo and so on.

At Level 2 the concept of corporate functional staff authority is introduced. Level 2 staff authority develops, introduces and enforces corporate requirements. The development of specific rules, procedures and requirements calls for specific expertise. For example, to develop a uniform chart of accounts for the entire organization calls for a depth of knowledge in accounting, budgeting and financial reporting. Such expertise is a requirement for corporate functional staff authority.

The recognition of functional staff authority changes the view on staff-line relationships. Line executives make operating decisions. Functional executives make decisions

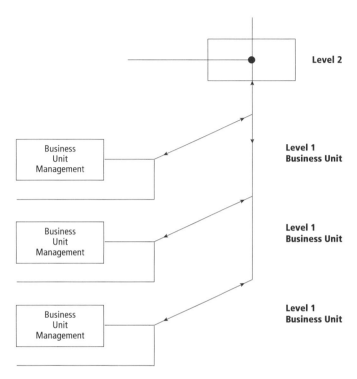

Figure 3. Level 2 corporate integrating mechanism

to introduce general requirements to be followed. Previously a staff person was viewed as an advisor who does not make decisions (like a kibitzer in a card game). The concept put forward here changes these kibitzers into responsible decision-making managers. They are both line and staff. When they participate in the top management decision process or make specific decisions in their own functions, they are line officers. When they interpret or advise, they are functioning as staff officers.

There is another important point to emphasize here. All requirements included in the corporate integrating and regulating mechanism relate not only to all business units, but also to all personnel at corporate headquarters including the top executives. The requirements apply to everyone and are used by everyone.

The corporate integrating mechanism is shown in Figure 3. This mechanism includes:

- routinized information flow to and from the business units
- corporate functional regulation—procedures, protocols, rules, guidelines, policies, operating standards, accounting and budgeting requirements, key indicators and so on
- shared corporate services—the pool of resources and capabilities available to the business units at their request

Level 3.
Corporate Business Management

Many corporations have a chief operating officer (COO), a title that sounds much like Level 3 Corporate Business Management. But the COO function may or may not be a true Level 3 in the system model of the enterprise. The system model Level 3 is responsible for the overall effectiveness and efficiency of the firm's entire operating system.

A System Model for Corporate Management

The top management of a large industrial firm found the expression "corporate operating management" a contradiction in terms. Something is either corporate or operational, they said. Another company's top management did not believe that a chief corporate operating officer could do things that a good chief financial officer (CFO) could not do. I had to show that a CFO deals with history while a COO manages the ongoing total dynamic business process. To clarify Level 3 in some instances, I switched the title from COO to corporate business portfolio monitor.

I believe that top management has difficulty in accepting this concept because it is a departure from financial control to true corporate direction. Corporate business management focuses on the organization's total operating system and carries out functions that cannot be handled by the management groups of the business units.

In my consulting practice I observed corporate chief operating executives who believed that their main task was to intervene in the operations of the Level 1 profit centers. This amounts to interference into matters in which they had no competence. In my view, developing specific business strategies for a business unit calls for competence in that business—a black box beyond the competence of corporate management. Yet corporate management would go much further than strategy formulation and interfere in many other detailed activities.

Why do corporate operating officers do this? Most likely they do it because hands-on involvement in business unit activities is easier than carrying out the true corporate functions of managing the total system formed by the business units. This corporate job is a highly sophisticated, conceptual and practical task.

Following are examples of the corporate business management functions:

- accomplishing globalization (division of work on an international scale)
- managing the business portfolio, bridging corporate- and business-level planning
- appraising the results of the individual businesses
- identifying new opportunities from the ongoing business activities
- identifying and fostering the corporate technological core competencies
- launching corporate-wide operating programs, such as total quality and agile manufacturing
- monitoring current business problems of corporate importance and creating inter-business teams to solve them
- setting corporate standards
- determining the boundaries (markets) of the operating units
- ensuring the sharing of expertise among operating units (e.g., by rotating people or by creating project teams)
- acting as tiebreaker in debates between operating units

- acting as a depository of business experience and knowledge
- building a culture of trust and voluntary communication among the operating units

Level 3 management discharges its responsibilities through three of the system model's communication channels:

- business channel
- integrating channel
- direct personal communication channel

Level 3 is illustrated with its communication channels in Figure 4. Level 3 is expected to use all three communication channels in a balanced manner. Experience shows that bureaucratic management tends to overload the integrating channel. Autocratic management tends to overload the business channel. And if management does not like to make decisions, it tends to use the direct personal communication channel for delaying the decision making or hoping that the need for decisions will go away.

Level 4.
The Management of Corporate Future-Related Activities

All viable companies are able to adapt themselves to ever-changing requirements. The adaptation process can take place in a variety of ways. Some companies accomplish it with the help of a planning department or by occasional

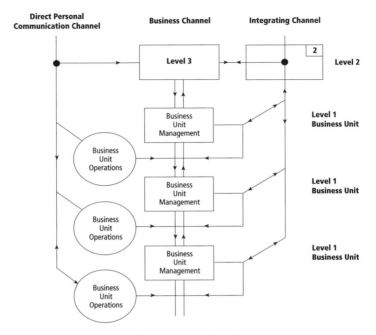

Figure 4. Level 3 corporate business management

special studies; others by special task forces, the use of outside consultants, special projects or by other means. In the system model of corporate management, Level 4 is the center of activities for innovation and adapting the organization to new requirements.

At the corporate level these activities aim at the achievement of survival and growth of the corporation as a whole. Similar activities are carried out by the business units' Level 4s for the business units' scope of activities. Corporate future-related activities include:

- corporate research and development
- acquisitions and mergers
- financial and personnel planning
- development and management of corporate projects
- development of corporate plans
- corporate resource allocation
- corporate look-out post activities, including such activities as trend tracking, industry studies, fundamental market research and technology forecasting

Corporate future-related activities are carried out by each member of the top management team. The team discusses fundamental planning and development issues, perhaps in a corporate executive committee meeting, but individual team members are responsible for contributing to such discussions and, later, for implementing plans.

The place of Level 4 in the organization is shown in Figure 6.

A proper balance must be maintained between the management efforts spent on directing the ongoing business system (Level 3) and the management of the corporate future-related activities (Level 4). When Level 4 activities are neglected and all efforts are concentrated on maximizing the short-term profitability of present businesses, over time the corporation will stagnate, fail to adapt to changing requirements, will not grow and eventually may go out of existence.

Level 5.
The Highest Management Authority of the Corporation

The highest level of management is more than one key position. Level 5 is the top leadership of the organization, made up of the board of directors, president and CEO and, usually, a corporate executive management team (see Figure 5).

The board of directors is the governing body of the organization. It exercises governance over management by carrying out the following functions:

- representing and ensuring the interests of the stakeholders (shareholders, customers, suppliers, employees, communities, government, environmental representatives, etc.)
- appointing management
- determining the basic context (i.e., direction, resource endowment, bylaws) within which management should direct, organize and conduct the business activities of the entire business system

Once management is appointed, the CEO is the highest management authority. But this level of management is not exercised alone. The members of the corporate executive management team are part of it.

Although the members of the corporate executive management team report to the CEO, the actual management process is characterized by a continuous flow of interaction among the team members.

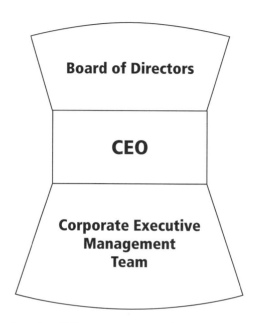

Figure 5. Level 5 corporate executive management team

The management process is organized to enable this level of management to exercise the overall leadership role. Its functions can best be described by presenting the entire model (see Figure 6), which so far has been discussed in parts.

Five points about this model should be emphasized:

- In terms of the model, corporate management can now be defined as Levels 5 + 4 + 3 + 2. In practice, the heads of the business units (Level 1) are typically members of a corporate operating committee. In this capacity they also are part of corporate management.

Those business unit executives who are members of a corporate operating committee are acting in a double capacity: as corporate Level 5 officers and also as Level 5 chief executives of their own organizations. Corporate management includes the top corporate management team, the corporate staff and the management support system designed to assist this level of management.

- The top management team can be structured in a number of ways. Note that the members are not only staff people, but responsible senior corporate line officers. Each has specific functional responsibilities, but the number one task for each member is the contribution to the top management decision process.

- Typically, Level 5 does not use the business communication channel. Instead, it monitors Levels 2, 3 and 4 and through them directs the entire organization.

- In cases of emergency, information goes directly and immediately to the CEO. The emergency channel, however, should be used only for true emergencies. Otherwise, management by crisis would prevail. A good example of this channel in use occurred during the Exxon Valdez oil spill in Alaska's Prince William Sound.

- It was stated earlier that the model is applicable to any level of management in a business organization provided that each level represents a business unit with three basic characteristics: a distinct set of operations, a distinct management and a distinct market

A System Model for Corporate Management

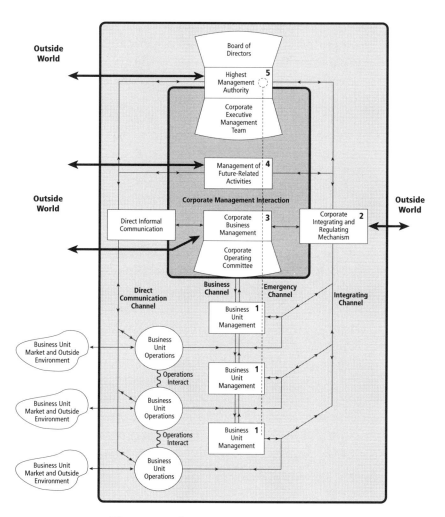

Figure 6. Corporate leadership system

(public). The model applies an important system notion called "the principle of recursion." According to this notion, in the world of systems, each system contains systems and is a part of a larger system. And the same model can describe each of these systems. Figure 6 portrays the application of the model to a total organization. In Figure 6, at the next lower level of recursion, each of the Level 1s could be described with this same model, each with its own Levels 5, 4, 3, 2 and 1.

This idea of recursion provides a new language for us. For instance, one can talk about Level 4 at recursion 1 (corporate headquarters), or Level 4 at recursion 2 (a business unit), or Level 4 at recursion 3 (a plant within a business unit). While all have Level 4 future-oriented functions, the scope and methods of management in each case will be very different. Each managerial recursion level has a decision-making role concerning those decisions that call for its vantage point and therefore cannot logically be made by higher or lower levels of management. For instance, at recursion 1 of a multi-business firm—the total business—corporate level strategies concern themselves primarily with the right mix of businesses and the synergies among them, while the Level 1 business units, recursion 2, worry more about the best way to compete in their industries.

In learning about system thinking and the system model presented in this book, many executives at first fear a loss of control. They're used to making decisions, asserting control. But in a system structure, decisions are made where they can best be made, and control is actually strengthened. Executives who like direct control will find that indirect control through system structure improves control throughout the enterprise.

In system terms, control is not something imposed from a higher level. Each unit is primarily self-organizing and self-controlling, with control an integral part of what is being controlled. The key idea in self-control is feedback from the work itself. Through the organization's structure of performance measures and key indicators, self-control is aligned to the achievement of unit and company purpose.

Each operating unit controlling its performance through feedback is not completely on its own. It is part of a larger system, the total company. In achieving its purpose it also contributes to the achievement of purpose of this larger system. This contribution is controlled by information flow in the three channels of communication shown in the system diagram.

Constructing the System Model

Looking at the organization as a system will help management understand and apply the concepts presented in this book. A first step is to begin with the existing, traditional organization chart. Then, through a process of dialog, testing and revising, the organization chart is mapped into a system model. The traditional organization chart shows who is where. The system model shows how the total organization works. It defines each of the five levels of the system and the information channels that integrate them. Figures 7 and 8 illustrate how this process works for a

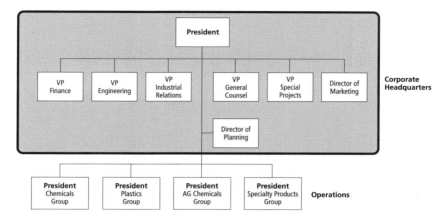

Figure 7. Organization chart of a large chemical products company

large chemical products company. Figures 9 and 10 illustrate the process for a large insurance company.

The system model can be used to appraise company strengths and weaknesses.[7] Such an appraisal is a useful way to learn about system thinking and the model, and their value to the company. Some of the weaknesses most commonly found in such appraisals are:

- System purpose is not clearly articulated and understood.

- System boundaries for the Level 1s are not defined or are defined inappropriately.

- Decisions are made in one system without an understanding of the consequences affecting other systems.

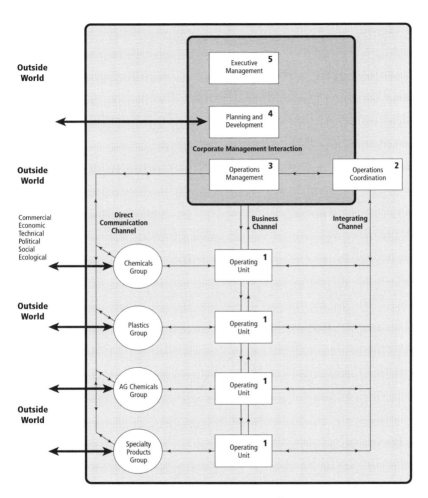

Figure 8. System model for the large chemical products company

- The Level 1s in their own operations are not using the disciplines inherent in the system model.
- There is no effective Level 2 communicating and monitoring corporate parameters and coordinating the relationships among the Level 1s.
- Level 3 is intervening in the Level 1s, making decisions that are better made within the Level 1s.
- Many of the Level 4 functions are not performed or are performed poorly.
- There is an imbalance in effort and investment between Level 3 and Level 4; usually too much in 3 (the present) and not enough in 4 (the future).
- Performance measures and key indicators are not appropriately thought out, communicated and used for change and improvement.

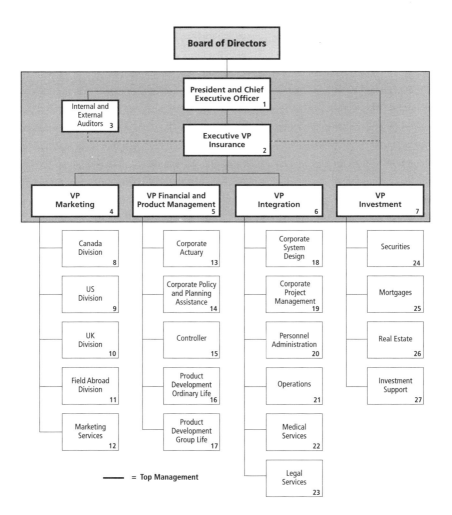

Figure 9.   Organization chart of a large insurance company (boxes are numbered to show where positions fit into the system model, Figure 10)

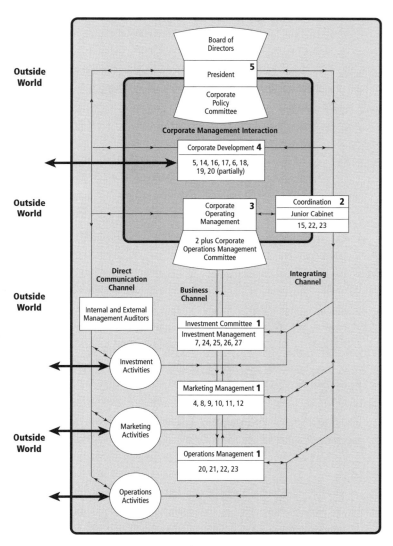

Figure 10. System model for the large insurance company

IV.

Corporate Management Role and Functions

CORPORATE LEADERSHIP IS EXERCISED jointly by the board of directors and the top management group whose members are appointed by the board. Typically the board exercises only particular key leadership functions—the governance functions. The management of the organization is left to the professional corporate management group. The board governs and management manages. This distinction strengthens the checks and balances of the decision-making process. Frequently one person will fill three job functions—chairman, CEO and president. In my opinion, this combination of functions weakens the leadership of the corporation.

Corporate management exists to discharge the corporate leadership functions. These functions need to be articulated and fully understood for at least three reasons:

- There must be an agreed-upon view about the functions of corporate management (remember the various perceptions described earlier).

- Each member of the top management group is responsible for the entire organization's total results and is accountable for certain functions.
- The responsibility referred to in the previous item calls for interaction and thus an understanding of the basics of all functions.

The role and functions of the top corporate management group are summarized below. This summary is based on my observations of the management practices of various corporate management groups, the notions of system science that can be applied to complex business organizations, and views developed from my studies and experience. Naturally the functions of a given corporate management group will depend on the perception of that group regarding the nature of corporate management, the particulars of the business activities involved and the choice of a management style.

Role

Corporate management designs, integrates, directs and monitors the total business system of a corporation formed of self-managed operating units. The corporate senior executives are appointed by the board of directors and act within the context set by the board. A top corporate management team under the leadership of the CEO discharges the basic functions of corporate management.

Core Functions

Corporate management has twenty basic core management functions. These functions are discussed in separate sections below.

1. Informing the Board of Directors

The top management team keeps directors informed about the state of the corporation and the implementation of board decisions.

2. Designing the Enterprise

Designing the enterprise includes the following:

- defining the company and the operating units
- designing the business infrastructure
- designing the management process
- establishing the network of corporate indicators
- directing the mechanization and automation of the work of the organization

3. Establishing and Maintaining the Top Corporate Management Team

Top management establishes and maintains a top corporate management team with each member acting in at least three capacities: (a) as a participant in the top decision-making process, (b) as a corporate executive overseeing one business segment and (c) as a functional officer exercising functional staff authority in a particular field. In the case of a global company, a fourth capacity may involve overseeing the business activities of a geographic area.

4. Personnel

Top management recommends the appointments of senior corporate executives, appoints headquarters staff and the heads of the operating units, ensures succession and carries out personnel development programs.

5. Development

The development function includes an ongoing effort to adapt and develop the organization for survival and growth. This effort includes divestments, acquisitions and mergers; research and development; and organization and personal development.

6. Monitoring the Ongoing Business

This function includes an ongoing effort to provide corporate operating direction to the corporation's total existing business system.

7. Finance and Administration

This function includes finance, treasury, taxation, risk management, accounting and administration.

8. Corporate Synergy

Top management identifies, fosters and utilizes the synergetic capabilities inherent only in the total organization.

9. Resource Endowment and Resource Allocation

Top management provides resource endowment to the operating units and withdraws resources or allocates further resources to the units as the business situation requires.

10. Financial Incentives

Top management establishes and maintains a financial incentive system both for corporate headquarters and the operating units.

11. Information Flow

Top management determines the corporate key indicators and assures an adequate routinized data flow centered around these indicators.

12. Functional Staff Authority

Each member of the top management team is accountable for providing corporate regulations for a dimension of the total business that applies throughout the company.

13. Corporate Core Competence

This function involves the preservation and further development of the core capabilities on which the company builds its success; inducing and ensuring the transfer of technology and other capabilities among the component units of the company.

14. Ethical Values

Top management determines the corporation's ethical values and conducts a continuous effort to ensure that these values are the values of all company people.

15. Compensation

Top management determines compensation levels for the headquarters staff and the heads of operating units.

16. Management System

Top management develops and maintains a corporate management support system.

17. Contractual Agreements

Top management enters into contractual obligations on behalf of the total organization.

18. Representation and Promotion

Top management represents and promotes the organization to the outside world.

19. Tiebreaker

Corporate management acts as a tiebreaker in debates between the operating units.

20. Managing the Corporate Headquarters

The top management leadership team has the responsibility for all of these core functions. Figure 11 illustrates how these functions are distributed among the top management team of the large insurance company shown in Figures 9 and 10.

Corporate Management Positions

Each of the top management positions shown in Figure 11 has an important, basic role.

Chief Executive Officer (CEO)

The CEO is the highest authority in the management structure and the chief designer of the total enterprise. He or she is the liaison with the board of directors and is accountable for the overall performance and position of the company.

Chief Operating Officer (COO)

The COO position can also be described as the corporate business portfolio manager (CBPM), with the general responsibility for everyday management of the ongoing, total business system. The COO watches closely the performance of the Level 1 business unit managements

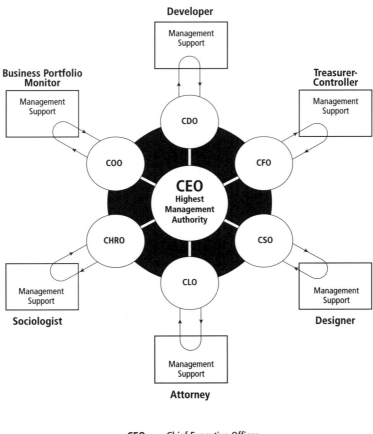

Figure 11. Top management leadership team of a large insurance company

and the effect of this performance on the corporation's business portfolio, taking actions as appropriate. The COO participates in and implements decisions for entry into new businesses and divestitures of others, and collaborates closely with the CDO in the implementation of strategic decisions.

Chief Development Officer (CDO)

The CDO position is responsible for managing the corporation's future-related activities, including the discovery of developing threats and opportunities in the market and other environments, and the formulation of appropriate corporate projects and actions. This function is an enhancement of the typical research and development and corporate planning functions.

Chief Financial Officer (CFO)

The CFO manages corporate financial planning; directs and measures the results of the company's monetary operations, taking actions as may be appropriate; and manages corporate administration, which provides good services to the corporation's stakeholders.

Chief System Officer (CSO)

The CSO is accountable for overall corporate integrity through integrating linkages and an information system that provides adequate and timely information flow. The CSO provides system design expertise to organizational units, assisting them in developing applications and in utilizing shared corporate services.

Chief Human Resource Officer (CHRO)

The CHRO position is identified as the sociologist. The CHRO focuses on the human element in the processes of the corporation. He or she exercises functional staff authority over human resource matters throughout the organization.

Chief Legal Officer (CLO)

The CLO assures that the corporation fulfills its legal responsibilities. He or she represents the corporation before legal authorities and carries out the organization's litigation activities. An important function of this position is the continuous study and analysis of changing interpretations and practices, and new and prospective legislation, keeping members of the organization informed, and determining any appropriate actions.

Summary and Conclusions

The question, "What is corporate management?" can be answered conceptually, in system terms and functionally.

The Concept of Corporate Management

Corporate management is a distinct level of management responsible for the overall results and position of an organization as a whole. It does things that cannot be done by the management of the component business units. It produces added values. A business system as a whole has capabilities that are inherent only in the total organization and are not possessed by the parts. Furthermore, certain decisions can be made only by corporate management if suboptimization is to be avoided.

The System of Corporate Management

The system model of corporate management does three things:

- It identifies a total organization in terms of corporate management and operating management.
- It describes the corporate management process in terms of a five-level systemic hierarchy.
- It identifies the communication channels between corporate and operating management.

In the systemic hierarchy, at Level 1 are the business units, the basic component operating units of the corporation. Level 2 contains the corporate integrating and regulating machinery. Level 3 is the corporate-level leadership and direction of the business units. Level 4 is the focal point of all future-related activities. Level 5 is the highest management authority of the corporation. The system model applies the principle of recursion, as discussed earlier, in which each system contains subsystems and is contained in a larger metasystem. The model presented therefore can be used to describe any management situation providing that it satisfies three basic requirements: a distinct management, a distinct operation and a distinct market. For example, the models shown in Figures 6, 8 and 10 to describe a total company can also be used to describe a Level 1 business unit, which in turn has its own Levels 5, 4, 3, 2 and 1.

Corporate Management Functions

Corporate management is responsible for the overall performance of the total business system. It directs, integrates and monitors the management of the component business units. A distinction is made between the functions of the board of directors and the functions of corporate management. The board governs and management manages. The corporate management core functions can be defined and explained in terms of twenty basic corporate management functions.

V.

Projects

THE FIRST FOUR CHAPTERS DISCUSSED corporate management and the usefulness of a five-level system model for organizing and managing the organization to achieve intended performance results, now and in the future. Levels 1, 2 and 3 conduct the ongoing day-to-day work of the organization, achieving objectives and continuously improving. Level 4 deals with future-related activities—the changes and innovations that will be needed for future success. Level 5, the top executive authority, provides direction and leadership for both the present and the future.

This chapter deals with the important Level 4 function of projects. Projects bring about the changes needed for future success. Projects are a responsibility of Level 4 in the corporate model and also at Level 4 in lower-level systemic recursions—subsidiary, division, profit center or plant. The Level 4 in each such subsystem defines and conducts projects for that organizational unit.

As you read this chapter, think about your organization with its ongoing operations always aiming to achieve desired goals and to continuously improve. And then add the "futures," those interventions that bring about needed change. These are "projects." How projects are defined and managed is a major management task in creating the organization's future.

Senior management must ensure that the right projects are worked on, and that the total effort and resources required for all projects are within the organization's capability. Senior management must also establish the right balance between ongoing business operations and new undertakings. This means that projects require two levels of management: top management direction of all projects, and the management of each individual project.

Following are fifteen basic project management requirements.

Corporate Management Requirements

- All defined undertakings must be subject to a project management discipline.

- The managerial situation must be conducive to the generation of project ideas.

- A project should be directly linked to managerial planning.

- Projects should be directed toward corporate goals.

- Project approval authority must be defined by various levels of management.

- Project approval and resource allocation must be two aspects of the same decision.

- An organization with many projects needs a project center to provide corporate direction for project management.

Specific Project Management Requirements

- Projects must be defined in terms of their ultimate purpose.
- Projects should be planned and implemented in stages.
- The chain of events of the project life cycle must be spelled out in advance.
- The participants and their roles in the project life cycle must be clearly stated.
- A distinct approach should be used for evolutionary and for innovation projects.
- Projects should be carried out with a team approach.
- Project progress should be reported on for resource utilization and degree of completion.
- Coordination between the tasks of a project and between projects must be based on the principle of self-coordination.

These project management requirements describe projects conducted at the corporate level. The same list can be used to describe project management requirements for a lower-level unit by substituting the name of that unit for the word "corporate." The following sections offer a few comments on each of the fifteen requirements:

Corporate Management Requirements

1. *All defined undertakings must be subject to a project management discipline.* Experience shows that in many organizations, as much as 40 percent of staff effort is spent on projects without this work being defined and managed as projects. The distinction between projects and operations must be understood. A project is a defined undertaking with a beginning and an end to be executed by a fixed date for a specific purpose. An operation is a repetitive, ongoing activity that lends itself to management, target setting and resource allocation. There should be a minimum level of importance and effort for an activity to be defined and managed as a project; otherwise, an undesirable proliferation of projects would occur.

2. *The managerial situation must be conducive to the generation of project ideas.* Project ideas may originate anywhere in an organization. Excellent organizations encourage and reward these ideas. Management can encourage project proposals by:

    - offering visible management support and publicity
    - providing rewards for accepted proposals
    - considering project proposals in promotion decisions

- providing time and money to certain people and groups for unstructured experiment
- encouraging project proposals in specified areas

3. *A project should be directly linked to managerial planning.* Projects are the practical means by which changes in direction, changes in the infrastructure of the business, changes in products and processes, and changes in the organization are achieved. Projects are not approved once a year in an annual planning process. They are submitted for approval whenever the project proposal is timely. Managerial planning must support this ongoing process.

4. *Projects should be directed toward corporate goals.* All projects should have a defined purpose. This purpose must be related clearly to the achievement of corporate goals. In practice, projects are often defined relative to the perceived needs of specific departments or organization units. It must be clear that in serving these needs the project is also supporting the achievement of overall organization goals.

5. *Project approval authority must be defined by various levels of management.* In a large organization, projects are defined and conducted at various levels of management—at the Level 4 activities of the

total organization and at the Level 4s in the organization's subsystem units. This provides a structure of projects throughout the organization, enabling the total company, and each of its component units, to make the continuing stream of changes needed for their future success.

6. *Project approval and resource allocation must be two aspects of the same decision.* Approval to proceed with a project must also include the resources needed for effective project execution. Project approval includes approval of the project definition and goal, the project plan and the project budget.

7. *An organization with many projects needs a project center to provide corporate direction for project management.* Projects are part of the Level 4 future-related activities by which an organization adapts itself to new conditions. Experience has shown that a "corporate project center" is the most effective way to direct the many projects to the needs of the organization and to provide support services to the various projects.

Specific Project Management Requirements

8. *Projects must be defined in terms of their ultimate purpose.* The purpose of a project is to satisfy a need for a customer or user. For example, a project's purpose might be to improve process X to six sigma quality and cut cycle time in

half. Or the purpose might be to commercialize Product A to achieve sales of $250,000 in year 1 at a contribution margin over 50 percent. Service departments in the organization should define their contributions as tasks of projects instead of viewing their contributions as projects themselves.

9. *Projects should be planned and implemented in stages.* Planning and scheduling a project by stages provides managerial checkpoints for determining the appropriate next steps, and approving or modifying the project plan and schedule. Typically deliverables are specified in advance for each checkpoint. Each checkpoint, then, is a go, no-go, or go-with-changes decision point. The stages of projects (such as a feasibility study, for example) should not be considered as projects themselves but as elements in the project plan. The same project manager should manage the project through all stages of the project. Figure 12 illustrates the planning of projects in stages.

10. *The chain of events of the project life cycle must be spelled out in advance.* Projects are planned in stages (see previous requirement). Within stages they are specified in terms of the events needed to complete the stage and provide the deliverables for the next checkpoint. Each event can be a review point and a decision point for the project team, for ongoing management of the project. The design for the life cycle of the project (stages

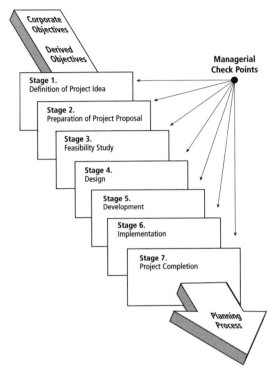

Figure 12. Project planning in stages

and events) should be included in the project proposal.

11. *The participants and their roles in the project life cycle must be clearly stated.* A project may involve the following participants:

- a project sponsor, who is an executive involved in the project and who represents the project at the executive level

- a project manager, who is accountable for organizing and managing the project
- steering committee members, who review and approve project work by stages
- team members, who are individuals assigned to the project
- a business manager, to whom the project manager reports
- an executive, who approves the project
- peer partners, who consider the merit of project proposals

The key person for project success is the project manager, who must have the ability, enthusiasm and commitment to make the project succeed.

12. *A distinct approach should be used for evolutionary and for innovation projects.* The purpose of an innovation project is significant change—something new and different; for example, launching a new business. The purpose of an evolutionary project is incremental change in existing activities. The organization of an innovation project requires far more freedom for participants than evolutionary projects require. Innovation projects need experimentation, ingenuity, flexibility and discovery. A flexible plan is needed, one that is developed as the work is done.

13. *Projects should be carried out with a team approach.* Self-managed teams are the best approach. Working within the broad constraints establishing the project, the project team:

- plans the project to achieve the purpose of the project
- plans and carries out, or directs, the events needed at each stage of the project
- informs and coordinates with sponsors and other company people and groups involved with, or affected by, the project
- listens to, learns from and communicates with the project customer(s)
- makes full use of each team member's capabilities
- drives all project events and stages to a successful, on-time completion

Only self-managed teams can accomplish all these. Working in a self-managed project team is a doing, learning, fast-growth experience.

Projects often transcend the boundaries of any one department, function or business unit. For project success, a multiunit, multidisciplinary team is needed. The number of team members, however, should be kept to a minimum. Figure 13 illustrates the relationships that are created in establishing a project team. Each team member

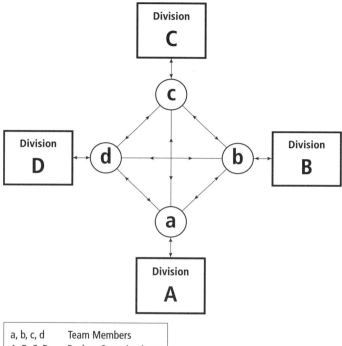

| a, b, c, d | Team Members |
| A, B, C, D | Backup Organizations |

Purposes of the team:

1) to achieve interaction between relevant activities
2) to achieve concurrent planning
3) to facilitate self-coordination

Notes:

a) Team member a has access to A but it is not a representative of A.
b) The number of the team members must be kept within manageable limits. Formula for calculating the number of relationships: $n(n-1)$. In this case we have 12 relationships: $4(4-1)$.

Figure 13. Interdisciplinary team approach

has a two-way relationship with all others. It is very desirable to select team members knowledgeable in more than one discipline.

14. *Project progress should be reported on for resource utilization and degree of completion.* The project reporting system has three basic objectives:

    - to provide information to higher-level management
    - to provide information to all organization units so that through self-coordination they can contribute to and support the projects
    - to provide a means for the project manager to control the project

15. *Coordination between the tasks of a project and between projects must be based on the principle of self-coordination.* The device by which self-coordination can be achieved is feedback. Feedback is information from the work itself that provides information to team members on any deviations from desired performance so that corrections can be made while the work goes on. Management is full of feedback loops. All project team members must be aware of the importance and the use of feedback, and feedback loops should be designed into the project work process. Self-regulation can be built into the project work process through:

- interaction between the project team and management
- adequate information flow on project progress
- design of the project life cycle
- continuous communication with the project's ultimate user or customer

Audit

The fifteen management requirements can be used to audit an organization's project management capabilities. Figure 14 illustrates an example of this kind of audit.

To conduct this kind of an audit, an explanation of the fifteen requirements as they are summarized in this book can be given to individuals working on project assignments. Then, after some discussion of the requirements, each person can be invited to rank the company's performance on each requirement, using the audit form shown in Figure 14. From all the responses, the median point is then calculated for each requirement, and this point is plotted on a copy of the questionnaire form, as illustrated in Figure 14.

It is also useful to give to management groups this questionnaire form and the explanation of the fifteen requirements. Although individual responses will vary, such audits provide a learning experience and can indicate where change and improvement may be needed.

Requirements	Low				Evaluation				High	
Corporate Management Requirements:	1	2	3	4	5	6	7	8	9	10
1. All defined undertakings must be subject to a project management discipline.						6				
2. The managerial situation must be conducive to the generation of project ideas.						6				
3. A project should be directly linked to managerial planning.					5					
4. Projects should be directed toward corporate goals.							7			
5. Project approval authority must be defined by various levels of management.				4						
6. Project approval and resource allocation must be two aspects of the same decision.						6				
7. An organization with many projects needs a project center to provide corporate direction for project management.	1									
Specific Project Management Requirements:	1	2	3	4	5	6	7	8	9	10
8. Projects must be defined in terms of their ultimate purpose.							7			
9. Projects should be planned and implemented in stages.						6				
10. The chain of events of the project life cycle must be spelled out in advance.					5					
11. The participants and their roles in the project life cycle must be clearly stated.							7			
12. A distinct approach should be used for evolutionary and for innovation projects.								8		
13. Projects should be carried out with a team approach.						6				
14. Project progress should be reported on for resource utilization and degree of completion.							7			
15. Coordination between the tasks of a project and between projects must be based on the principle of self-coordination.					5					

Figure 14.   Project management audit

VI.

Summary and Conclusions

THE SYSTEM CONCEPTS AND MODEL described in this book can be extremely useful to managers at all levels, in all kinds of organizations. Any business can be modeled using this kind of a system model. The process of developing the model and then using it in day-to-day operations can very much focus and simplify management practices and strengthen operating results.

Some of the benefits commonly experienced in the management process of developing and using a system model and system concepts include the following:

- clearer and more effective definition of the Level 1 operating units, and the purpose and mission of each
- significant improvement in the Level 2 coordination of the Level 1 operating units
- more (and better) decisions made at lower levels
- less interference from the corporate level in Level 1 operating unit decisions

- great improvement in the Level 4 future-related activities
- more time and talent devoted to system design and management of the whole, especially to clarifying purpose and mission and developing and using information feedback loops on key performance measures
- great improvement in the company's information system flowing through the three communication channels

Developing and using a system model and systems concepts at each level of recursion (corporate, subsidiary, division, profit center and plant) can result in these kinds of benefits. The model can be used at each level to assess the current situation. Then ongoing use of the model and system concepts can help management create the organization's capability for survival, growth, profitability and the delivery of superior values to customers and other stakeholders.

Some of the changes that have resulted from using a system model and system concepts:

- An annual budget and planning cycle is eliminated. With the company's purpose and structure established, the process of monitoring the model plus the Level 4 future-related activities maintains and adapts the system. When a budget or profit plan is wanted it can be produced at any time as a read-out from the model. Dialog, then, can develop any needed changes.

- Each level does its own planning with no need for passing planning documents between levels.
- Participation and dialog become important elements in the communication process through the three communication channels.
- Control is less imposed from a higher level. Each level is primarily self-organizing and self-controlling through feedback from the work itself related to desired performance objectives.
- The financial model as traditionally used for management control becomes one element in the overall system model.
- Monitoring the system model, with its information flow among all system levels and with the outside world, enables the organization to learn and to evolve toward the achievement of its purpose.

With these benefits, and these changes, we see indirect control providing more effective control than can be accomplished with direct control. All the elements in all the organization are coordinated and self-managed to accomplish desired performance results. The chain of command is unchained. But control is strengthened. And results improve, both in the present and for the future.

Conclusions

1. Taking charge of corporate leadership includes the responsibility for positioning, developing,

integrating and monitoring the corporation as a total business system.

2. An organization has integrity if all the component operating units contribute to the achievement of the purpose of the total business system. All viable systems have a degree of integration.

3. There is a difference between decentralization and self-managed operating units. The former is still part of a traditional, hierarchical management structure, and the decentralized unit depends on the existence of the corporation. Self-managed operating units, in contrast, could survive on their own. They are linked into the corporation by integrative means rather than the chain of command.

4. The structure of a system determines the connectivity, communications and performance of its components for an overall purpose. The corporate structure can be visualized as a system model.

5. The typical organization chart describes a mechanistic, bureaucratic organization. Transposing this traditional chart into a system model can help management develop a more adaptive, enterprising organization.

6. Indirect management sets the context within which the operating units conduct their business. This context is established by corporate

SUMMARY AND CONCLUSIONS

parameters. From the standpoint of an operating unit, a corporate parameter is an independent variable that has to be observed and followed. Corporate parameters are developed, introduced and enforced by corporate functional staff authorities.

7. There is an important distinction between point-to-point decisions and functional decisions. A point-to-point decision is the decision of a superior given to a subordinate in a specific matter. A functional decision regulates and integrates on an across-the-board basis and does not make decisions in specific matters. The former centralizes and interferes; the latter sets the context for organization activities.

8. The principal players of the corporate leadership are the members of the board of directors and the members of the top corporate management team.

9. The board governs and management manages. Governance includes the following functions:

    - safeguarding the interests of the corporation's stakeholders
    - appointing management
    - establishing the context (direction, resource endowment and bylaws) within which corporate management should conduct business activities

Corporate management manages the enterprise as a total business system and carries out the twenty management core functions described in Chapter IV.

10. Informed decision making by the top corporate management team of a large international organization calls for adequate consideration of at least five basic dimensions of the business:

    - the current and long-term business performance of the total corporation
    - the current and long-term performance of the component business units
    - functional requirements
    - the market situation
    - networking by the team with each other and the management of the business units

11. A systems approach to the organization of the top management team would include these seven members:

    - Chief Executive Officer (CEO)
    - Business Portfolio Monitor (COO)
    - Developer (CDO)
    - Treasurer-Controller (CFO)
    - Designer (CSO)

Summary and Conclusions

- Sociologist (CHRO)
- Attorney (CLO)

12. Operating unit management can use the same system model and system concepts as shown and described for corporate management, applying each of the five levels of the model to the unit's scope of operations.

The most important conclusion is that by using system thinking, corporate management can unchain the chain of command, improve company performance and concentrate its efforts on "managing the whole" for success today and—with changes as needed—for tomorrow.

APPENDIX: VSM

Figure 15 shows Stafford Beer's pictograph of the Viable System Model (VSM). Dr. Beer explains that the cybernetic research embodied in the VSM demonstrates that control is a disseminated function of the interaction of the parts of an essentially self-organizing system. Control and other functions result from these systemic interactions. The structure of the system controls the system.

Corporate integration is achieved by homeostatic interaction on six identifiable vertical channels. The useful understanding of this depiction of the VSM, Dr. Beer points out, requires awareness of the cybernetic concepts of complexity and variety; the all-important law of requisite variety; and the concepts of relative autonomy, recursion, closure, identity and cohesion.

All of these concepts are explained in Dr. Beer's books, *Brain of the Firm, The Heart of Enterprise,* and *Diagnosing the System for Organizations.*

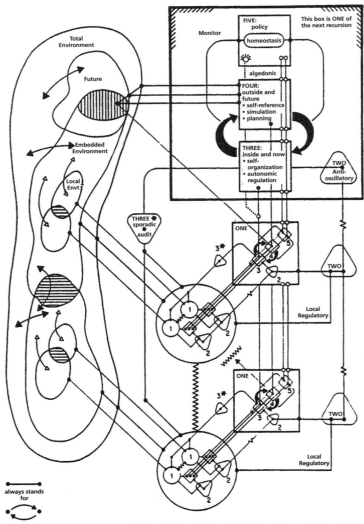

Source: Stafford Beer, *Diagnosing the System for Organizations,* John Wiley & Sons, 1985, p. 136. Used with permission.

Figure 15. Stafford Beer's Viable System Model (VSM)

REFERENCES

1. Burnham, James. *The Managerial Revolution.* New York: Penguin Books, 1942, p. 38.
2. von Bertalanffy, Ludwig. *General System Theory.* George Braziller, 1968, Foreword, pp. xv–xvi.
3. At a conference of the International Society for System Sciences. The Society's headquarters are located at the College of Business, Idaho State University, Pocatello, Idaho 83209. Basic system science references include: von Neuman, *Game Theory,* 1947; Wiener, *Cybernetics,* 1948; Shannon, *Information Theory,* 1949; Beer, *Managerial Cybernetics,* 1956; Simon, *Hierarchy Theory,* 1957; Churchman, Ackoff, & Arnoff, *Operations Research,* 1957; and von Bertalanffy, *General System Theory,* 1968.
4. *Brain of the Firm,* McGraw-Hill, 1972; *The Heart of Enterprise,* a companion volume to *Brain of the Firm,* John Wiley & Sons, 1979; and *Diagnosing the System for Organizations,* a companion volume to both of these books. New York: John Wiley & Sons, 1985.
5. Koestler, Arthur. *The Ghost in the Machine.* London: Pan Books, 1967, p. 48.
6. Ibid., p. 343.
7. Beer, Stafford. *Diagnosing the System for Organizations.* New York: John Wiley & Sons, 1985.

Further Reading

Beer, Stafford. *Brain of the Firm.* New York: McGraw-Hill, 1972.

Beer, Stafford. *The Heart of Enterprise.* New York: John Wiley & Sons, 1979.

Beer, Stafford. *Diagnosing the System for Organizations.* New York: John Wiley & Sons, 1985.

Chandler, Alfred D. Jr. *The Invisible Hand: The Managerial Revolution in American Business.* Cambridge, Mass.: The Belknap Press of Harvard University Press, 1977.

Drucker, Peter F. *The Frontiers of Management.* Truman Talley Books, 1968.

Koestler, Arthur. *The Ghost in the Machine.* London: Pan Books, 1967.

About the Author

Over a career of more than four decades, Paul Rubinyi served in management positions under the communist regime in Hungary, and then in government and free-market firms in North America and Europe.

His academic background includes Ph.D. degrees in economics and in managerial cybernetics, and a Diploma in accounting. He considered himself a generalist and believed in the need to draw from a broad knowledge base to successfully manage large, complex organizations. He did not consider management a science but believed that a broad knowledge of the sciences, and especially systems science, is needed for managing today's complex organizations.

Dr. Rubinyi was familiar with corporate management practices both in market economies and in planned economies. His occupational history included ten years in management positions in the communist government of Hungary. After emigrating to Canada in 1957, he studied accounting, earning his Chartered Accountant Diploma. He held positions as corporate planner in a large mining firm and as director of planning for a large government agency. With the Canadian consulting firm of Ernst & Whinney for twenty years, he became partner in charge of a senior management consulting service. He then established his own consulting practice offering counsel and assistance to senior corporate executives.

Dr. Rubinyi worked with many large firms and government organizations in Europe and in North America applying the concepts and methods described in this book. He was working on the manuscript for this book at the time of his death.